You Have Rights!

Elizabeth Anderson Lopez

What Are Rights?

You have rights.

A right is something that a person is allowed to have, get, or do.

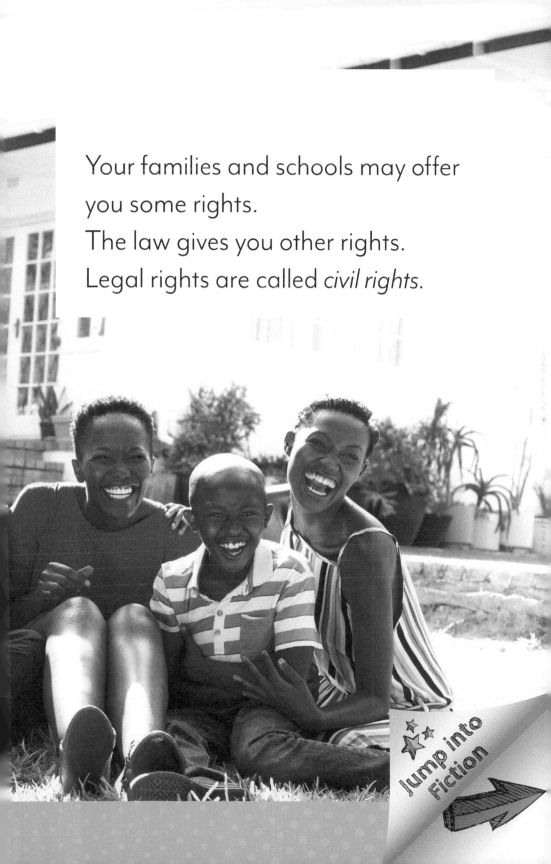

Your families and schools may offer you some rights.
The law gives you other rights.
Legal rights are called *civil rights*.

Jump into Fiction

Helping Owen

Owen wheels to the ramp and stops.
A branch is blocking the ramp.
Rose knows Owen needs help.
Owen has the right to get into the
school and learn!

"Owen, do you need help?"
Rose asks.
"Yes, please!" Owen says.
Rose picks up the branch.
Owen thanks her and goes into
the school.
He is ready to learn!

Back to Nonfiction

The Right to Learn

Young people have the right to learn.
It is the law in the United States!
It is one of many civil rights young
people have.

Think and Talk

Why is learning a right?

Going to school is a basic right. Students may learn about their other rights in school as well. They can learn how to protect their rights too.

Students learn to write in school.
Then, they can write letters to
their leaders.
They can ask leaders to protect
their rights.

Families have some options about where kids learn.
They have three main choices in the United States.
The choices are public school, private school, and home school.

When Home Is School

Children may go to school at home.
This is called *home school*.
But they still have homework in
home school!

Equal Rights

Rights should be equal for all students.
For example, at one time, only girls
could take cooking classes.
Only boys could take building classes.
It was not fair.
This has changed!

Equal Sports

School sports have to be equal too.
Sports are for all kids.
That is the law.

Schools must have tools for students.
States have laws about this.
Public schools get money from states.
Private schools are paid for by the families.
School leaders spend the money on what
their students need.

Some students need extra help. These students have the same rights as all students. Schools must help them learn in the way that is best for the students.

Stand Up

Learn to stand up for your rights.
Learn to help other people stand up
for their rights too.
People have rights. Our rights matter.

Speak Up!

If someone tries to take away your rights, tell someone in charge.

Civics in Action

All people in the United States have rights. Your rights cannot be taken from you. This is the law.

1. Make a list of your rights.

2. Circle the one that is most important to you.

3. Make a poster to show that right. Use words and pictures to tell why the right matters.